THE SPIRIT OF

VW

50 REASONS WHY WE LOVE THEM

Vaughan Grylls

BATSFORD

CONTENTS

INTRODUCTION

The Spirit of VW

This is not a technical book. It is about Volkswagen, a German company that, more than any other car manufacturer, has led the development and quality of European design and engineering and been at the forefront of its successful export throughout the world.

It started in 1934 with the idea of a car for the people. The German Chancellor, Adolf Hitler, instructed engineering professor Dr Ferdinand Porsche to design a car for Germans who couldn't afford a car. Apart from being cheap to buy through savings stamps, it had to be economical to run, utterly reliable, hold a family of five, be air-cooled so you didn't have to garage it in winter to avoid the engine freezing up, and be capable of zipping along Germany's new autobahns at top speed all day. Nothing like this had ever been done before. It was a tall order, although Porsche had blueprints to go on – a proposed car designed in 1925 by Austro-Hungarian Béla Barényi, and advanced designs by German-Jewish engineer Josef Ganz.

The car that Porsche put into mass production was called the KDF Wagen or 'Strength Through Joy Car'. Thanks to the Second World War, production switched to military versions: first the Kübelwagen, followed by the Schwimmwagen, the purpose of which speaks for itself.

After the war, the largely ruined VW factory found itself in the British zone of occupation. A British army officer, Major Ivan Hirst, was put in charge of the site. The name of the location of the factory and the town for its workers became Wolfsburg, named after the nearby Wolfsburg Castle.

The KDF Wagen, advertised in the 1930s.

Hirst tried to tempt each of the British car manufacturers to take VW off his hands as war reparations, but not one was interested. Said their joint official report: '... the vehicle does not meet the fundamental technical requirement of a motor-car ... it is quite unattractive to the average buyer ... To build the car commercially would be a completely uneconomic enterprise.'

Hirst eventually found the answer in his deputy, the former manager of a pre-war Opel factory, Heinz Nordhoff, who had hated the KDF Wagen, regarding it as an unattractive yet dangerous rival. Nordhoff would make the Beetle, or Bug as it became known in the US, the most successful car ever, with over 21 million built.

How did such an ugly little bug become the motoring smash hit of the world? Four reasons:

Firstly, it wasn't expensive.

Secondly, it was built to a superior standard of strength, finish, reliability and longevity. Most cars, apart from the very expensive, felt flimsy by comparison. They just couldn't match that satisfying clunk when you shut your VW's door.

Thirdly, the German-invented autobahn. The VW was originally designed to cruise at 62mph (100 km/h), but by 1953, thanks to a slightly increased engine size, it could hammer away all day and night at up to 70mph (110 km/h). Top speed was autobahn cruising speed. No car, other than the most expensive, could do that. Why? Simply because, as there was no autobahn network outside Germany, there was no call for a cheaper car to be able to do it. In 1958 Britain even a mid-market car, such as a Morris Oxford, was only designed to tootle along at around 55mph (88 km/h), with an occasional burst of speed, just enough to overtake groaning lorries on the country's narrow roads.

Lastly, VW's success was built on its astonishing penetration of the crucial American market – the first foreign car manufacturer to achieve this. Volkswagen's advertising agency's witty approach to selling the VW in the US became the Madison Avenue benchmark for brilliance.

Yet by the early 1970s, VW's reliance on its flagship Beetle and its air-cooled derivatives was running out of road. Although VW's glamorous cousin, the niche Porsche, would continue with air-cooled, rear-mounted engines until 1997/98, it was time for VW as a mass-producer to face the fact that the spread of autobahn networks outside Germany had led to the development and mass-production of reliable, high-performing conventional cars that were cost-effective and far more pleasant to drive. And, most worryingly, Japanese cars were starting to best VW in the US market.

The signs came early. By the late 1960s, cost-cutting measures appeared. To address decreasing profit margins, economies had to be found that did not compromise VW's legendary build quality. Upholstery now only came in black, while bright fittings inside and out began to disappear. It was as if VW's cars were returning to their pre-war utilitarian origins.

Eventually VW had to grasp the nettle – the phasing out of air-cooling and rear-engine mounting. In 1973, VW launched the Passat, a mechanically identical car to their Audi 80 (VW had acquired Audi in the previous decade), which had been unveiled the previous year. It was sold as the successor to VW's Type 3 and 4 sedans. But the world was waiting for the big one, and this was something VW simply could not dodge. In 1974 VW launched the Beetle's replacement – the Golf (the Rabbit in the US) – while holding its breath, because this could be make or break.

They needn't have worried. The Golf was also a smash hit. It replaced the Beetle as Volkswagen's iconic car. Although there would be many me-too examples from rival manufacturers, especially of its Golf GTI and R models, the Golf led the field.

In 2015, VW had to hold its breath again. The diesel emissions scandal almost engulfed the company, especially in the litigious United States. There were mass demonstrations, including at VW's Wolfsburg headquarters. On the world stage, Germany, with its standard-bearing Green Party, was embarrassed to say the least. VW's cheating on testing its diesel cars was inexcusable in anybody's book.

Why was VW berated more than the others? After all, it was not the only manufacturer blatantly breaking the rules. Two reasons – the Volkswagen's economic clout meant it represented post-war Germany. And VW produced cars designed and built with honesty in mind. A Volkswagen did what it said on the can. But this time it didn't.

Kraftwerk on stage, 2009.

VW has since turned the corner, and now produces some of the world's most interesting electric cars. Recently they announced that the Golf will go the way of its predecessor, the Beetle, as an all-electric world beckons. Yet that relentless quality will undoubtedly remain. No wonder one of Kraftwerk's best concerts took place at the Wolfsburg factory. Think Autobahn. Think VW.

Because it is so large and successful, VW is more vulnerable, paradoxically, to the politics of external relationships than any other manufacturer in Germany. For example, Russia's attack on Ukraine has affected the import of Russian natural gas, meaning that VW's main power station in Wolfsburg cannot switch from using coal as planned. More seriously, VW has a longstanding and immense investment in China, now supplying over 50 per cent of the company's profits.

Today, VW takes turns with Toyota as the world's most successful automobile manufacturer ever. Its range of cars and models, the car companies it owns and the number and size of its manufacturing plants across the world is truly awe-inspiring.

And here are 50 reasons why we love VW ...

01

THE VW IMAGE

Here is a picture of a VW Golf GT Syncro taken some time in the 1980s, when every photograph in the world was now in living colour. Yet this is in black and white, making it appear on the arty side.

Is this just a pic of a car in a landscape with a woman in the mid-distance riding a horse beside a lake? I don't think so. What we have here is a scene of timeless tranquility.

The horse hints at pedigree breeding ... and maybe its rider does too.

Everything is classic, understated and quality.

In one shot, the VW image.

The VW Golf GT
Synchro, 1980s.

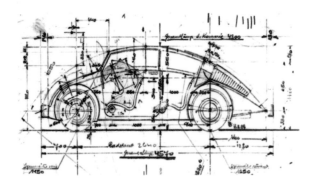

02

VW DADS

Who invented the Volkswagen? It depends where your gaze falls. In the 1920s, a time when Germany was in the financial doldrums thanks to First World War reparations, it must have been galling to look across at countries such as Britain, where the working classes were graduating from bicycles and motorcycles to Austin Sevens, while in the USA everyone seemed to be whizzing around in Model T Fords. Both models had been designed as cars for the masses.

In Germany, the rich had their Horches and Mercedes, just as the British had their Rolls-Royces and the Americans their Cadillacs and Cords. But there wasn't much economic motoring choice in Germany for those who could only afford a motorcycle.

In 1925, Béla Barényi, a precocious 18-year-old technology student from Hungary, came up with a cracking design that would have been cheap to build. It had a streamlined body, rear-wheel drive and an air-cooled boxer engine. It didn't reach production because in 1923 there was no money at all in the pockets of those it was designed for.

Above left: Plans for the Standard Superior model. Above right: Béla Rarényi. Opposite: The Standard Superior, 1933.

But along came a brilliant auto-engineer, Josef Ganz. He would design
a car, the Standard Superior, with some of these characteristics. And
it was actually produced, if only in small quantities, from 1933 to 1935.
Ganz's problem was that he was Jewish, and in 1933 he was arrested
by the Gestapo on trumped-up charges of blackmail – probably
encouraged by jealous rivals in the German auto industry. Ganz fled
Germany the following year, the same year German Chancellor Adolf
Hitler instructed a professor of engineering, Dr Ferdinand Porsche, who
headed his own Stuttgart design company, to come up with a car for the
people. The professor found one, inspired by you-know-who. Porsche
then designed the factory to build the car.

Left: Ferdinand Porsche
with the KDF Wagen.
Above: The 1938 launch
of the KDF Wagen in
Nazi Germany.

The engine, an air-cooled, four-cylinder, horizontal-opposed, was actually designed by Franz Reimspiess, an Austrian engineer who worked in Porsche's studio. (During the war Reimspiess was Germany's main tank designer; the formidable Tiger tank was one of his creations. After the war he was design engineer for Porsche cars.)

The unveiling of the KDF Wagen in sedan and soft-top versions in 1938 was the mother of car launches. Nothing at the Frankfurt Motor Show has ever matched it. How many of these delighted supporters actually ordered one of these cars, we shall never know.

Then there is the photograph of the KDF Wagen in downtown Berlin. It was taken supposedly in 1938, but judging from the blackout masks on the headlamps, used throughout the Second World War, it could be later. Standing next to it is Ferdinand Porsche. With this car the professor gave Hitler what he was looking for. Yet failure may not have been an option, which could account for his grim expression. The sign above the licence plate can be translated as 'venture attempt' or 'dare to try'.

Today the professor would look more cheerful, for the Porsche family own a controlling interest in the huge VW Group. They still keep a watchful eye on what VW does, even supplying some of its chairmen and directors.

VW and Porsche are family, and always have been.

03

A CAR FOR THE WORLD – EVENTUALLY

The KDF Wagen could be bought through savings stamps, and although many Germans entered the scheme, they didn't have the time to save enough stamps or receive their car thanks to the war, when output was diverted to military requirements. After the war, several tried to get their money back from the re-established Volkswagen company, or at least have their stamps applied to a post-war Beetle. That didn't work either because the Reichsmark, on which the stamps had been based, was replaced in West Germany by the Deutschmark. East Germans, of course, didn't even try.

The images here show how the KDF Wagen was marketed in Germany before the Second World War. A young couple camp beside a lake. They marry and have a pretty house and a blond child whose favourite toy appears to be another version of strength through joy – a howitzer. Then there is a holiday (we are looking at the suitcases) in a capacious KDF Wagen. Lastly, they meet a couple who perhaps are in the stamp scheme too. If so, they have their own car to look forward to.

Unfortunately, none of this ever happened.

Der Innenlenker

Opposite and below:
Advertising images for
the KDF Wagen, 1930s.

Fahrgestell und Aufbau des KdF.-Wagens weisen bei Vermeidung alles Über-
flüssigen jene harmonische Zweckmäßigkeit auf, die für Fahrer und Insassen
auch längere Reisen angenehm machen. Die Verlegung der Sitze zwischen die
Achsen ergibt eine nahezu unveränderte Schwerpunktslage, gleichgültig ob der
Wagen mit dem Fahrer allein, oder mit fünf Personen besetzt ist, und rückt alle
Sitze in die Zone bester Federung, die jedes Rad unabhängig von dem anderen
schwingen läßt. Seitenneigung des Aufbaues in Kurven ist restlos vermieden.

04

THE WORLD GETS THE BUG

It is astonishing how the VW Beetle caught on, especially given its Nazi history.

How did that happen? Well, it didn't break down (at a time when most cars did), it was quite inexpensive, it was beautifully screwed together, and it was unassuming – even though it could pound relentlessly along interstates, autobahns and motorways all day. And let us not forget, VW's advertising was brilliant, especially in the US (see also pages 88–91). The Bug was also fortunate in America, because it didn't have other European cuties as competition, such as the cool British Mini. They had been banned on crash-safety grounds. Ouch!

Here are two German punters in the late 1940s or early 1950s with their new car. This is a post-war Volkswagen and not a KDF, even though it has the split rear window, which was dropped in 1952/53. The chrome hubcaps complete with VW logo, another VW logo just below the windshield, the bright fittings scattered throughout and the Wolfsburg emblem at the front show this to be an early Nordhoff car.

Left: The VW Beetle at the North Miami Beach Love-In festival, 2020. Opposite: The VW Beetle in the late 1940s or early 1950s.

Its driver is trying to figure out how it all works and why. Being German-logical, he first consults the car manual. Is there some amusement, as well as bemusement, on his face?

And here are two American punters at the North Miami Beach Love-in event in November 2020, fondly revisiting their 1960s hippy past. Less bemusement. More amusement.

The Bug was noisy, challenging in cross-winds and in the wet, and had hopeless headlights and wipers. As for the so-called heater, it was often jammed on or off – on in the summer and off in the winter. Of course.

Despite this, VW's signature car (and its camper van) brought a smile to the face of the world. The world was on its side. The Bug had been got.

Opposite, above:
Beetles on the
production line in the
1950s. Opposite, below:
ID.4s on the production
line in 2022.

05

RELENTLESS QUALITY

Nobody did quality control better than Volkswagen. In fact, that was one of the concerns when VW decided that the Beetle's days were over, because by the early 1970s, all the car had left going for it was quality control and build quality.

Here they are in 1954 at Wolfsburg in West Germany, being turned out at a rate of 900 every day. All production lines look relentless, but this one looks totally totalitarian. (I thought that was East Germany's schtick.) Dumping the Beetle and switching to modern-looking cars could have meant that modern-looking quality control would result. Just think of all those British Leyland mid-1970s cars.

It didn't happen. The Golf, the Polo, the Passat and all their derivatives were still much better put together than rival offerings. Which is a big reason why people bought them.

Here is the VW ID.4 production line today. Relentless quality lives on. It has to. Because the rivalry now comes from Japan, South Korea and, increasingly, China.

06

BEETLING OFF

In 1972, VW were at the top of their game in America. They sold 423,000 Bugs, the highest they had ever achieved into that market. It was also the best-selling car in the US that year. Yet VW were already planning to phase it out, certainly in the European market, where, unlike in America, performance and handling were now at least as important as robustness and reliability.

In 1974, the last regular Beetle left the production line in Wolfsburg. Here it is being given a fond farewell by its makers. Limited production continued at Emden, West Germany, until 19 January 1978, when the last car went straight to VW's Autostadt museum in Wolfsburg. The cabriolet version would continue to be hand-built in Europe by coachbuilders Karmann until model year 1979/80.

Opposite, left: The last Beetle off the Wolfsburg production line, 1974. Opposite, right: The last Beetles made in Pueblo, Mexico, 2003. **Above:** Pope John Paul II's Beetle in the Vatican Museum.

Yet the Beetle was not quite dead, for production continued outside Europe. It wasn't until 2003 that the very last Beetle, known as the Vocho in Mexico, left the line. Given the roads, robustness was king for longer in Latin America. Here are the final cars getting a loving polish at the VW plant in Pueblo, Mexico.

Should you seek immortality, even for a Beetle, look no further than the Vatican. Here in the carriage pavilion of the Vatican Museum is the last dazzling white Vocho, presented to Pope John Paul II by the President of Volkswagen Mexico on 26 May 2004.

07

THE MAGIC MICROBUS

Can you think of any cooler set of wheels than what is called the Transporter, the Microbus, the Camper, the Van, the Bus? Whatever?

Whatever? A teenager's favourite word, but also a word that epitomizes the lifestyle of those who see themselves as doing their own thing outside the mainstream. Frenetic is uncool, laid-back is cool. Slow is cool. Hence the popularity of the Bus.

It was dubbed the Type 2 by VW because the Beetle was the only other model VW made before this was launched in 1950 as a van, the Kombi and the Commercial. For a decade, from 1964, VW also built the Fridolin, a Type 147 panel van for postal services, etc. That wasn't so cool. It would be the Type 2 that was. Definitely. Here were cool lifestyle possibilities beyond mere utilitarian and commercial considerations.

The Type 2 had the same engine at the back as the Beetle and the same wheelbase but, given its solid body, it was *slowwww*. Yet it could go anywhere, so there were two cool reasons to buy one. Here is an early split-windshield classic model (the Splitty) in a suitable get-away-from-it-all setting.

It was followed by the T2 of the Type 2 in 1967. Called by everyone the Bay Window, or just the Bay, thanks to its wide-screen windshield, it was stronger and heavier and so the engine was larger. Alongside the Beetle itself, the T2 continued with more powerful engines to choose from until 1979.

The split-windshield VW Microbus.

I had a 1973 T2 van that I bought in 1975 when I was doing up my first house. I loved it, and when the doing-up was done, I sold it to a friend who lived in about the most remote part of Wales you could find – that's if you could find it – several miles from a paved road. He kept it – and lived in it – for a decade.

The word 'Type' would be dropped from the Bus as a designator to avoid confusion with VW's Type 3 and 4 cars. VW called them just T, followed by the number. The Type 2's successor was thus called the T3, or Type 25 in the UK, for some obscure reason. It was launched in 1979 with an air-cooled engine, but as with VW's ditching of air-cooled models almost everywhere else, conventional petrol and diesel engines were fitted, the same with the T4 from 1990, the T5 from 2003 and the T6 from 2015.

Automatic transmission became an option, although choosing that meant losing a sensation many of us loved – a warm, comforting feeling of slowly stirring porridge when what we were actually doing was changing gear.

These later Buses were very good drivers, especially the T6, and versions such as the California are extremely well-appointed. But achieving cult status? About as likely as the 'New Beetle' launched in 1997. Anyway, here is a painting advertising the T4 to the Love Generation, which had long since passed.

Lastly is an ID Buzz Electric Microbus, all ready for the future, assuming there are charging facilities in those remoter parts where any adventurous owner would surely plan to venture.

Right: The VW T4.
Below: The ID Buzz
Electric Microbus.

08

FAMILY SEDANS

An array of suitcase-engined VWs.

By the end of the 1950s, when the West German economy was taking off (helped largely by VW's export success), Germans were wondering why they couldn't drive round in something that looked more like, you know, a regular automobile with room for the family and luggage, but as robust and reliable as the Beetle on their driveway.

In 1960, VW came up with the answer, called, of course, the Type 3. There was now a trunk at the front, a trunk at the back and, in the US, a young Dustin Hoffman employed on a VW commercial puzzling over where to find the engine. It was still in the back, still air-cooled, but now under the trunk floor – flattened so successfully that it became known as the suitcase engine.

Here is a line of suitcase-engined cars, discounting the Beetle at the front and the K70 at the back.

There were three different rear ends to choose, from the notchback, the fastback for those who wanted something a bit sexier, and the squareback station wagon, called the Variant outside North America. The two beyond are Type 4s. We will come to those later.

The Type 3 had a 1500cc (later a 1600) engine. The orange car on page 34 is a 1972 fastback, one of the last of the breed. The Type 3s were pensioned off in 1973, to make way for the water-cooled, front-wheel-drive VW Passat – dubbed the Dasher in the USA.

What were the Type 3s like to drive? Pretty good, actually. They would cruise all day at 85mph (135 km/h), astonishing in the late 1960s and early 70s for a mid-range car. I went through five Type 3s – a notchback, two squarebacks and two fastbacks – all very reliable, except the second fastback. As I was on my way to work one morning, sitting in London traffic next to a stall full of rare books, my fastback caught fire.

All this, plus 5 people...

REAR BOOT

FRONT BOOT

(Equipment by courtesy of Selfridges Ltd.)

there's only *one* car they could have

They insisted on a sports car. With twin carburettors, leaping acceleration, and a cruising speed of at least 85 m.p.h. ☐ But then there was all that luggage. So it had to be a sports car with estate car room in the back – plus more room in front, under the bonnet where others keep their engine. ☐ A tall order? Not to Volkswagen, who make just such a car. A 5-seater, tough, dependable, with all the well-tried VW features. So versatile, it just had to be called the Variant. Try it for size!

VW VOLKSWAGEN
WEST END SHOWROOMS: 34 DOVER STREET, LONDON W.1. TEL: HYD 1881 • HEAD OFFICE: ST. JOHN'S WOOD ROAD, LONDON N.W.8. TEL: CUN 6000

I didn't realize what was happening because the engine fire was, well, in the back. Two panicking rare booksellers made me pay attention.

The fastest Type 3 I ever owned was a 1966 Variant 1500S. You can see an ad for one here. That car had real go – up to 120mph (190 km/h), believe it or not. Astonishing, especially for such a sedate-looking conveyance.

The last VW air-cooled sedan was the Type 4, introduced in 1968 as a larger Type 3. You could order it as a squareback or a fastback. There were two generations, the 411 with a 1700cc engine (1968–72) and the 412 with the same engine initially but from August 1973 an 1800cc engine (1972–74). Here is a yellow 412 dating from the last year of manufacture.

The Type 4s were roomy cars and, like all VWs, were solidly put together. This was the last attempt to hang on to air-cooled, rear-wheel drive in a VW car. Indeed, they were the only European four-door air-cooled cars available.

As an aside, the Brasilia, a bland-looking, yet bizarre amalgam of upright Beetle engine, Karmann Ghia chassis and Type 4-inspired body, continued to be made in Latin America until 1982. Even VW does bizarre-bland occasionally.

09

MOVING WITH THE TIMES

Here is an NSU Ro80. It is quite a looker, isn't it? Designed in 1967 by Claus Luthe, it was way ahead of its time. The power plant was sensational – a twin-rotor engine designed by Felix Wankel. In 1968 the Ro80 was awarded Car of the Year.

VW bought NSU in 1969, merging it with Auto Union to establish Audi. But then things started to go out of kilter. The Wankel engine was unreliable, and there were bodywork problems. Naturally, this was all rather embarrassing for VW, whose reputation was based on build quality and reliability.

VW soldiered on with the Ro80, before folding it in 1977. But the one-time Car of the Year did not entirely die, for its sleek looks influenced the Audi. There was also NSU's conventional water-cooled version, called the K70, also designed by Claus Luthe. (The Ro took its name from 'rotary', the K from *kolben* ('piston').

The NSU Ro80.

But things were now getting confusing. VW regarded the K70 as a successor to their Type 4 cars, but there was the Audi 100 which overlapped with the K70, if not with the Type 4. Was mighty VW losing the plot? Their dealers must have been puzzled.

Looking back at these strange times, a psychologist would pronounce, 'displacement activity'. Because all this NSU Ro80, Type 4 and K70 stuff was fiddling around the edges. The elephant in the room was when and how VW was going to replace the Beetle.

My mother had a K70 for a couple of years. I drove it once from London to Paris and, yes, it was underpowered for a car of its size and its fuel consumption was poor. But it drove well and it was comfortable. So I feel rather sad that such a good-looking, advanced design bit the dust.

Yet VW had to make the K70, and it is good they did so. Because it paved the way for their successful future.

The VW K70.

10

THE MIGHTY GOLF

Throughout its existence, Volkswagen has pumped out many models and it continues to do so. Yet in our imagination, there are only two VWs so far. The Volkswagen Beetle and the Volkswagen Golf. Icons both. Everything else is a variation, other than that hard-done-by and long-forgotten K70.

But can you imagine the sleepless nights in Wolfsburg in the run-up to the Golf launch? Here was a car that would be totally different to its predecessor.

Mechanically, yes. But was it really? If you ever see a Mk1 Golf today, you will notice that it is no bigger than a Beetle. And not only that, it is about as utilitarian. No unnecessary decoration. The Mk1 was solid and it did what it said on the can.

And yet there is more to why the Golf saved Volkswagen so quickly. Yes, it was a brilliant car. But what about the millions of us who had held a real emotional loyalty to that noisy, quirky Beetle? We had bought more of them than any other car in history. So, in our millions, we were on the Golf's side. We willed it to fill its predecessor's shoes. And it did, especially by offering variations, such as the Jetta with its trunk.

What else in the Beetle influenced the future development of the Golf? Subtle evolution. Just look at the Mk1 and Mk2 GTIs. Completely different body panels but still cleverly looking almost the same. Quite a feat to pull that one off.

Above: The VW Golf Mk1. Opposite, above: Mk1 and Mk2 Golf GTIs. Opposite, below: The Mk3 Golf GTI.

By the time the Mk3 and Mk4 came along in the 1990s, that angular look had softened. Golfs seemed less purposeful, less *statement*. Perhaps they were a victim of their own success, because by now, every competitor had their base versions of the Golf, right up to the GTI.

While we are on the GTI – okay, I'll admit it, a personal favourite – I'll just say what you already know: that the 'hot hatch', and more than any other the Golf GTI, pretty much killed off the European mass-produced sports car. Apart from the Porsche, of course, but that was family, wasn't it? And there is something even more significant. More than any other car produced by Volkswagen, the cracking performance, reliability, build quality and value for money of the GTI catapulted the whole VW brand into the premium bracket.

Above: Mk5 and Mk6 Golf GTIs. Opposite: The Golf Mk8.

The Mk5 and Mk6 Golfs reclaimed some of the laid-back coolness of the original, while the Mk7 accelerated the process, which would make it the go-to model for Golf nuts.

There is now the Mk8, launched in late 2019. And with so many choices – Variant, GTE, GTD, GTI, R – it is a head-scratcher to choose which is best for you. But whatever Golf takes your fancy, you won't really need any other type of car.

The R 20 Years Edition, built to celebrate 20 years of the mighty Golf, has a maximum speed of 168mph (270 km/h). Insane. Its even rortier successor is the limited edition R333. I write about these two on pages 126–129.

But that is the end of the line for the second most successful car in VW's history. Because the Golf name has ended. The future is all-electric.

VW's Beetle was classless, but it was never classy. VW's Golf was both. You could show up in it anywhere. Which was an important part of its genius.

11

PETITE POLO

Stealthily, we tend to pile on the pounds as we pile on the years. We move less as we get older, our metabolism is slower, and we can afford more restaurant visits. That's my excuse anyway.

It's the same with cars. But why should this be? Safety legislation means more weight? The buyer is less agile? The buyer has more spare cash as well as spare pounds? All that, but the fact is that no one is attracted to the latest model if it is a skinnier and smaller version of the car they already own. For whatever reason, today's VW Polo is a lot plumper than the first model, and it's even quite a bit plumper than the first Golf.

In the early 70s, VW used its upmarket Audi brand to dip a toe into the water-cooled, front-wheel-drive world. So it was with the Polo, launched in 1975 as a utilitarian version of the Audi 50, which had come to market the year before. In 1978, VW dumped the Audi because the Polo had killed it. Who wants a pricey econocar?

VW needed the Polo to compete in the new supermini market, then led by the value-for-money Fiat 127 and Renault 5. Other manufacturers soon crowded in with their Ford Fiestas, Fiat Unos, Peugeot 205s and Nissan Micras. We'll be kind and overlook the Austin Metro.

Seen on page 44 is a launch model Polo. Designed in-house, but with styling cues taken from the Golf – the rear-side window kink was the only Italian (Bertone) contribution – the Polo cost a little bit more than a Renault 5, but that wasn't a problem, because punters would pay a little bit more for legendary VW build quality. As for the Polo in what I'll politely call brown sludge, it is actually a long-forgotten Derby – a notchback version offered to those looking for a separate trunk. The name was dropped in 1984 and it was rebadged the Polo Classic.

I had a Derby in the early 1980s. My mother bought it for me. I hated it, passed it to my stepfather and vowed I'd never drive a Polo-type car again. After that it was just Golf for me.

Thirty years later, in a dark night at a Danish airport, I am collecting a rental. I soon discover it has that engine cutting-out thing at traffic lights,

Above: The VW Derby. Opposite: The Polo GTI on the Monte Carlo Rally, 2021.

something I hate. Yet in every other way, I admit this new Golf is brilliant. And the following morning, I find out it is a fifth-generation Mk5 Polo.

There have been many Polos and many models and names, usually the basis for cars built by VW's subsidiaries Seat and Škoda. How many times have you picked up a rental and thought, isn't that a Polo? But as you get nearer you see it is an Amio, Arosa, Cordoba, Fabia, Ibiza, Lupo, Playa, Rapid, Vento, Virtus or Vivo.

At the top of the Polo tree is the GTI. Here is one on the Monte Carlo Rally in 2021.

Yet like its big sister, the once petite Polo, with all its alternative brands, models and names, will disappear to make way for VW's ID.2. But at least their engines won't die at the traffic lights, because you won't be able to tell whether they are on or off.

12

PRAGMATIC PASSAT

The pragmatic Passat was the first VW front-wheel-drive, water-cooled engine car fully designed by the company. It was launched in 1973 as a variation on VW's Audi 80, which had hit the showrooms the year before. Here seemed to be a sensible, if somewhat dull, replacement for VW's Type 3 and Type 4. The good news is that nobody in Wolfsburg had their heart in their mouth when it was launched because these pragmatic sedans were not VW's bread and butter. This was not Beetle-Golf *High Noon* time.

The bad news was that this model was now up against cars such as the Renault 16, a brilliant mid-market family conveyance that had more or less destroyed VW's Types 3 and 4. Would it destroy the Passat?

At first the Passat struggled. It could not benefit from the loyalty and fair wind extended by all those Beetle nuts to the Golf when that was launched. But pragmatic Passat pulled through. And from then on there would be a bewildering number of models and names, each depending on when and where the car was made or exported to – Carat, CC, Corsar, Dasher, Magotan, Quantum, Santana. Yet Passats all.

This first-generation sedan in orange, called the B1 (no, not Carrot) is a 1974 model, designed by Giorgetto Giugiaro. By the way, VW went crazy on orange as one of those must-have early 70s colours. Think orange cushions and avocado bathroom suites.

The yellow car is a 1992 B3 Passat. It was almost a VW throwback, not having a conventional radiator grille. As for yellow, that had become the colour to have in the late 80s/early 90s. Think of all those cinema commercials and MTV videos featuring yellow Saab Turbo convertibles (perhaps the only model that ever made that company any money).

The red sedan is an eighth-generation Passat, a 2020 R-line model, designed for the US market and built at VW's Chattanooga plant. Sadly, this good-looking car didn't last long. In 2022 VW pulled the Passat out of North America because of poor sales – mid-size sedans and station wagons had had their day. They had been pushed aside by the any-size-you-like (usually large) SUV.

Back in 2003, I found myself in Canterbury at the time of the installation of the new archbishop, In the precincts of the cathedral, parked in a line, stood the official cars of the bishops of the Church of England, each shiny black and displaying a flag of their bishop's coat of arms. It was a most impressive sight.

The only grand automobile in the line-up was the conveyance of the Bishop of London, a 1950s Rolls-Royce. A few other makes made it, a Jaguar here, a Mercedes there. But one make and model was the most popular by far. The moral of the Passat is 'pragmatism with dignity'.

Here endeth the lesson.

Left: The VW Phaeton in production, 2010. Below: A Phaeton outside the factory it was built in, 2003.

13

POSH PHAETON

The Phaeton, a limousine-like car, was made from 2002 to 2016. It was the brainchild, indeed obsession, of then VW chairman, Ferdinand Piëch, a scion of the Porsche family, controlling shareholders of VW. Piëch wanted to stick it to Mercedes with their S Class and especially Lexus, whose design and build qualities were then worrying the European luxury car manufacturers.

Yet VW already had their Audi A8, not to mention Bentley, so why didn't anybody tell the chairman to forget the project and not be silly? I think we know the answer.

The benchmarks given by Piëch to his designers were that the car should be capable of driving all day at 186mph (300 km/h) through an exterior temperature of 122°F (50°C) while keeping 72°F (22°C) inside. Also there would be electric motors galore, hidden away, doing about everything you can think of. The Phaeton's platform would be shared with Bentley's Continental GT and Flying Spur models.

The car's fuel consumption was certainly not great but, despite the irony, a dedicated 'eco-friendly Transparent Factory' was built in Dresden to hand-build the car, as seen here. Here also is a 2003 Phaeton outside the eco-friendly plant that gave it birth.

The Phaeton's interior was the last word in luxury, making another irony of the 'people's car' logo on the steering wheel.

And therein lay the problem. True, VW had come to be seen as a premium brand. But it was not a luxury brand across its range. For the same money you could buy a marque that was – Mercedes, BMW, Lexus, Range Rover, Jaguar or indeed an Audi, which VW made anyway, not to mention a Bentley, which VW made also.

Quite simply, the Phaeton project was mad. In 2013 *The Economist* placed the Phaeton as one of Europe's biggest loss-making cars. Yet the German Chancellor, Gerhard Schröder, had one from 2002 to 2005. Why? Because it signalled 'man of the people' and prestige at one

and the same time. But punters tended not to be German chancellors or even run-of-the-mill politicians. And besides, there weren't enough rich eccentrics around to buy Phaetons in the quantity required for the company to turn a profit.

From the beginning the Phaeton's name signalled a warning. It wasn't an open light carriage from the Victorian age. Rather it was its Greek mythological namesake, Phaethon, who, in the face of warnings, drove his chariot too close to the Earth and then too far away. The stars didn't like it and complained to Zeus, who obligingly sent a lightning bolt in Phaethon's direction.

The Phaeton was an amazing car, and there were five developments of it. I'll admit to having hankered after any one of them. But then, I'm a bit eccentric. So I love VW for being, occasionally, a bit eccentric too.

14

COOL COUPÉ VW

VW makes laid-back, level-headed cars, from the Beetle to the
Microbus, and on to the Golf and now the i-range. Here are cool cars for
people who see themselves just like that. We are absolutely not 'Look at
me!' types. But cool coupé cars? We want them back!

The first VW Karmann Ghia, the Type 14, was launched in 1955. It was
designed by design company Carrozzeria Ghia in Italy, with coachwork
by Karmann in Germany. In my opinion, the Type 14 is one of the coolest
coupé cars ever to hit the road. Launched in 1955 as the second
passenger car designed after the Beetle, but with the same engine and
floorpan, it was an immediate hit, especially in America.

Was it slow for a coupé? Of course. It was a Bug, a Beetle in fancy
clothes. But the buyers it attracted didn't care one bit, because this
was a cool coupé for cruising around Beverley Hills or Menton on the
French Riviera. Whether you were actually in Beverley Hills or Menton
was beside the point. 'Look at me!' it said, wherever you went. In 1957, a
convertible was added. Here is one actually in Menton.

In 1962 another version, dubbed the Type 34, was launched. This was
based on the Type 3 engine and floorpan, and being larger was more
expensive. In fact it was the priciest car in VW's range. Sadly it wasn't
sold as a convertible or into the US, probably because for that sort of
money you could rock up in a Porsche. There was also this fastback

prototype, the TC 1600 (above). A version was built as the Type 145 in Latin America and sold there from 1972 to 1975.

After these Karmann Ghias, VW somehow lost the plot when it came to coupés. Look at this 1977 Scirocco, seen here with supporting flares. Why not buy a Golf GTI instead? Many thought so too. The same with this early 1990s Corrado VR6 Storm, billed a bit unthinkingly by *Car* magazine as one of the '25 cars you must drive before you die'. Scorching drive, but look at it. Sorry.

Then there were the concept coupés such as this 2009 BlueSport. Actually, I don't think it is all that bad when it comes to cool. Better than the over-styled 2015 Golf GTE Sport, which is far too shouty.

Can VW design a cool coupé today as they did with the Karmann Ghia all those years ago? Or did the Golf GTI and R kill off all attempts, because those were the cars we really wanted?

A colleague of mine once described our Type 14 Karmann Ghia as 'a triumph of aesthetics over common sense'.

He was right. And that was why we loved it.

Above: The prototype Karmann Ghia TC 1600. Opposite, clockwise from above left: The 1977 Scirocco; the 2015 Golf GTE Sport; the Corrado VR6 Storm; the 2009 BlueSport.

An abandoned Beetle
in Texas.

15

CUTE VW

In emerging economies, the classic VW Beetle was recognized as a tough, reliable workhorse. In the UK it had a more utilitarian image than the Mini, with just a little of the Mini's cuteness. But in the US, its main overseas market, the Bug was definitely cute. The seeds for that may lie in the 1960s tongue-in-cheek Madison Avenue advertising campaigns.

This Beetle lies abandoned near Highway 287 in Texas. It may have passed, but its spirit lives on, for today there are many former hippies and even some present ones who meet regularly to celebrate the alternative lifestyle for which the classic Bug as well as the classic Type 2 Bus continue to say, 'I am alternative!'

So it was no surprise when, where else but at Volkswagen's Design Center in California, they came up with a retro-themed, front-engined, water-cooled New Beetle in 1994. Designed by J Mays and Freeman Thomas, and based on the Polo's platform but then switching to the Golf Mk4, it was launched in 1997, with a convertible added in 2003.

As with other VW models, various editions were offered, such as the RSi, the Ragster, the Blush and the BlackOrange. This one is in tasteful green, well matched to its This England setting.

In 2011 VW launched a successor, calling it the A5 Beetle, but with other names for other countries, such as the Käfer in Germany and the Maggiolino in Italy. It was based on the Jetta, itself based on the Golf. Like its predecessor, there were lots of special editions, often

tying themselves to products of the classic Beetle's period, such as the Fender Stratocaster guitar. There was even a goofy 'Herbie the Love Bug' version, as well as 'Coasts and Waves', presumably in reminiscence of the Beach Boys. This one in Thailand is a #PinkBeetle, the only model that VW made to include a hashtag in its name.

In July 2019 VW ended its foray into the retro-cute market. That was sad because although these silly cars commodified alternative lifestyles – an example of a contradiction if ever there was one – they were huge fun.

So I think we should love VW for bringing genuine pleasure to those not here when the classic Beetle was itself clattering around, not to mention we oldies who were given an opportunity to relive our Love Bug past in a car less likely to go bang.

Opposite: The New Beetle, pictured in 1999. Above: The #PinkBeetle.

16

UP! VW

VW has a micro-mini called the Up! and, before we laugh, let it be
known that it won World Car of the Year in 2012. The Up! followed an
established VW tradition for 'citi' cars, although few of us today have
strong memories of the VW Lupo or the VW Fox.

The concept Up! had rear-engine, rear-wheel drive. Of course
everyone thought that very retro-sweet, but by the time it was launched,
VW had come to its senses and the Up! now had its three-cylinder one-
litre petrol engine up front.

The Up! was launched in 2011 and, of course, there were VW
subsidiary models – the SEAT Mii and the Škoda Citigo. There was also
an E-Up! launched in 2013. Lifestyle models beckoned, such as the
SEAT Mango, made with Spanish fashion house Mango in mind, and a
crossover model called, of course, Cross Up!

In the UK you could have a High Up!, Move Up! or Take Up! Also a
Black Up! and a White Up!, until someone at VW woke up and reversed
those pretty smartly to Up! Black and Up! White.

The Up! is sold in Europe, Latin America, South Africa and Japan,
where it is popular for buzzing about their busy cities. This blue one
screams perfect car for a car-sharing scheme. Here it is in Sofia,
Bulgaria, in 2021. The white one is a 2018 GTI on show at the Scary Cars
Assembly in Bicester, England, in 2022. It will do 122mph (196 km/h) and
has a six-speed manual gearbox. In early 2023, VW stopped making Up!
GTIs. Just a teeny bit too scary?

17

OFF-ROAD VW

VW has an impressive tradition for off-road vehicles, whether they were intended to go off-road or not. In fact, its first mass-produced item was the military Kübelwagen, seen here on a test drive with Dr Porsche and friends aboard. Then there was the floating version, the Schwimmwagen. Here is a GI trying out a liberated one towards the end of the Second World War.

They say that a classic Beetle will float. It has a sealed platform and doors that were so tight-fitting, it was a good idea to crack open a window before attempting to pull a door shut. In fact a 1960s commercial boasted: 'The VW will definitely float, but it will not float indefinitely.' Obviously the ad agency's lawyers had a hand in that sentence. Anyway, here is a Beetle swimming with its Schwimmwagen cousins.

Then there was the Type 2 Bus. They could go many places off-road thanks to their sealed platform and high ground clearance.

Opposite, above left:
Ferdinand Porsche test-driving the Kübelwagen.
Opposite, above right:
The Schwimmwagen.
Opposite, below:
A Beetle and some Schwimmwagens.
Above right: The VW Type 2 Bus.

Left: A VW dune buggy.
Below left: A Beetle setting out in the Sahara, 2005. Below: The Baja Bug VW Beetle, a scaled-up model of a toy. Opposite: The VW Touareg.

There are lots of variations on the dune buggy, first created by Bruce Meyers in California and called the Meyers Manx. They were mainly for funsters, which could occasionally mean annoying sunbathers on the beach. The ID Buggy will be more quiet about it.

The Bajas were a hit as kids' toys. In fact, the big ones are toys for big kids, sometimes called grown-ups. This marvellous blue Baja is a full-size replica of a kids' toy modelled on a full-size Baja. Figure that one out.

The yellow Beetle is fully prepped for racing across the Sahara, which is what it is doing here. Serious stuff. I would stick with a Touareg for Saharan use, and not just because they were named after some of the inhabitants of the place. This is a first-generation 2006/10 model. Introduced in 2003, the Touareg is some tough set of wheels. It has won a clutch of awards, including (embarrassingly) Least Green Car in America. If that troubles you, there is now a plug-in hybrid available. Astonishing to think that must mean charging points right across the Sahara. Really?

18

ELECTRIC VW

A challenge some car manufacturers face on going electric is what to do when they have an iconic radiator design. Just think Rolls-Royce and BMW. Have you seen the front end of BMW's electric offerings? Luckily, VW is not in that position because they didn't have a rad up front. That VW logo said enough.

In 2022 Hamburg, a smart-casual Thomas Schäfer, CEO of VW Passenger Cars, explains the ID.2all, which will form the basis for VW's small electric car to be launched in 2026. It will be around the size of the current Polo, have a 280-mile (450km) range and be capable of 0–62mph (0–100 km/h) in seven seconds, with a sports version to go faster. (By the way, ID stands for 'Intelligent Design'. That doesn't mean God for those who don't believe in white beards, etc.)

Then we move to April 2023 and the Shanghai Auto Show. Here is the ID.7 Vizzion. This large family car, with a claimed 435-mile (700km) range, is made at VW's plants in China. It is the forerunner of a concept

Above: Launch of the ID.2all, 2022.
Opposite: The ID.7 Vizzion electric sedan.

automobile, the ID.7 Space Vizzion, a Level 5 Autonomous that will have neither steering wheel nor dashboard. But there will be three rows of seats. Automobile in name and nature.

VW was the first foreign car manufacturer to conquer the China market. When I first travelled around that country in 1986, I saw few foreign cars, indeed few cars at all. Ten years later, Shanghai was awash with VW Santanas (Passats). Today VW aims its electric production at China, though it will have increasingly strong competition from China's home-grown products. Here in 2022 downtown Shanghai is a Volkswagen ID.Store, with one coming to you soon, if you live in China.

The other key market outside Europe for VW has always been the US. It still is. The ID.4 and ID.5 (the fastback version) are compact crossover cars. At the 2023 New York International Auto Show, the ID.4 shows off its electric underwear.

Last but not least is this photo of an ID.3 in the early morning, driving the empty winter streets of Helsinki, Finland. I think this is the best image for VW's new electric era.

Classic, timeless, cool VW.

Opposite, above: The VW ID. Store, Shanghai. Opposite, below: An early morning drive through Helsinki. Above: The ID.4.

19

WACKY VW

Wacky VWs speak for themselves and span the globe.

Here we have a marriage of a Type 1 Beetle with a Type 2 Bus at England's annual middle-class-let-your-hair-down Glastonbury Festival.

If you don't know whether you are coming or going, a self-styled wizard in New Zealand has created this red Type 1 Beetle(s).

And over in New York State is The Rat, created in homage to its many brethren down in New York City.

All are wacky and works of art.

Opposite, above: The
Rat. Above: A Beetle/
Bus hybrid. Right: A
push-me-pull-you Beetle.

E-Golfs on the
production line.

20

LOOK AT ME? DON'T!

Those who buy VWs don't like being stared at. Anonymity is the name of the game, coupled with that subtle signal of taste, the VW badge.

VW's huge output across the world ensures anonymity for those who drive them, a paradox that first became apparent when the Beetle became so ubiquitous, we didn't give them a second glance. Today the Golf. Tomorrow the ID range.

Here are some e-Golfs on a VW production line in Dresden sometime in 2017. To me this image represents that anonymity the typical VW owner seeks.

21

GO COMPARE

This is a splendid picture of a Mk7 Golf GTI Clubsport rubbing shoulders with the mighty of the car world in 2016. Other than the F-word on the left, most cost several limbs more than the GTI.

From left to right: Ford Focus RS, BMW M2, Jaguar F-Pace, Mercedes C63 M2, Audi R8 V10 Plus, McLaren 570S, Rolls-Royce Dawn, Porsche Boxster S and, tucked away at the back, our VW.

A fine array of cars,
pictured in 2016.

Above: A VW Beetle police car, Veracruz, Mexico. Right: An incident on the autobahn. Opposite: A VW police car in West Berlin, 1948.

22

POLIZEI VW

VWs have always been favoured by the police. Reliable, relatively inexpensive to run, good resale value, quite quick. Well, maybe not the drophead with its canvas doors, photographed in West Berlin in 1948. But how about those steel side-girders to alleviate scuttle-shake?

The Beetle kept going for quite a time in police employ. This one in Veracruz, Mexico was still cruising the streets in 2004.

And then there is an autobahn pull-over. Yes, it's our GTI and a €100 fine for exceeding 130 km/h (80mph). We had just driven into Germany from Switzerland, and I said to my wife. 'Let's open up this GTI!'

'Please don't. You could get caught.'

'Never. We are now on a German autobahn.'

Thus came the Passat Polizei. And the officer said, in perfect English before departing, 'You are lucky. If you had been in Switzerland or France, it would have cost you a lot more than that. If you want to go fast, you can 20 kilometres further on.'

I didn't. And my wife said nothing.

23

ICONIC VW

Question. When does a car become an Official Icon? Answer: When it lands in an iconic museum.

Here is me in 2014 at the British Museum, London, about to enter a superb exhibition: *Germany: Memories of a Nation*. This 1956 Beetle is placed at the entrance to set the scene. It is the same year and model of the car I first owned.

In 2019 a panel discussion called *Design to Move* was convened at the Museum of Modern Art, New York. They discussed the end of the Beetle's production and the future of VW design. Seen here from left to right are: Professor Rebecca Pailes-Friedman of New York's Pratt Institute; Paul Galloway, collections specialist at MoMA; Klaus Bischoff, executive director of Volkswagen Design; and Tamara Warren, journalist,

Above: A Beetle at MoMA, New York.
Opposite: The author at the British Museum.

author and moderator of the discussion. The VW is a 1959 model and has been dubbed 'Rita' in honour of Galloway's late mother, who drove a Beetle. This car is now in MOMA's permanent collection.

In 1999, Sonja Ticehurst holds an enlargement of the cover of the LP *Abbey Road.* The photograph was taken on Friday, 8 August 1969. Sonja is standing in front of Germany's Ahlden Castle, where the VW on her left is to be auctioned. This 1968 1300 is the actual car shown on the Beatles' cover.

The in-joke here, typical of the Beatles, is that the Beetle in Abbey Road could be a clever reference to the fifth Beatle, George Martin, who discovered the band and orchestrated their hits. LMW 281F is now in VW's Autostadt Museum, Wolfsburg, and is one of VW's proudest possessions.

The Beetle that appeared on the *Abbey Road* album cover.

24

CHIC VW

As a picture is worth a thousand words, I don't need to write anything more about this 1960s picture of chic, alpine elegance.

The 1500 Karmann Ghia coupé, around 1960.

25

VW GO BIG

If there is one thing that put VW way ahead of its European competition, starting it on the path to going big, it was cracking the American market.

Following the Second World War, the USA was by far the richest consumerist country on Earth. America was awash with vast automobiles that were growing longer every year. They were promoted as an essential part of the American Dream – a husband and non-working wife, two beautiful children, a beautiful house with all the mod cons and the latest Yank Tank – as the Brits enviously called them. Such automobiles were great for visiting other competing couples, even as grandparents, as seen in this 1957 'straight out of tomorrow' Mercury advert. The automobile you owned simply had to be the latest. This was the beginning of the age of built-in obsolescence.

In 1959, Volkswagen approached the Madison Avenue agency DDB (Doyle Dane Bernbach). Could DDB sell their Beetle into America?

Promote an ugly little car? With VW saying they couldn't stretch to colour ads, just black-and-white? It sounded ridiculous.

STRAIGHT OUT OF TOMORROW
1957 Mercury
WITH *DREAM-CAR DESIGN*

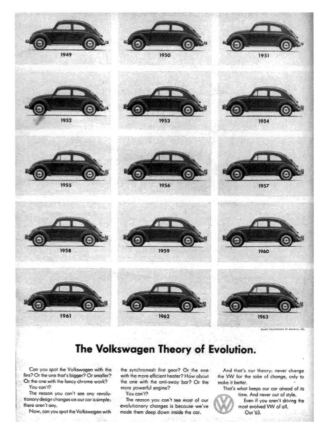

But then Helmut Krone, DDB's art director, got thinking. What if the drawbacks were the key? And so with the ad agency's copywriter Julian Koenig, Krone came up with ads that would become industry classics – *Think small* and *Lemon*. With equally brilliant ads to follow.

Unlike the typical American car ad, the VW ads did not present humourless fantasy. They presented humorous reality in black and white. These little cars were tough. They could drive all day at maximum speed on America's new interstates. They didn't break down, and if they did, they were cheap to repair. And the kicker was you didn't have to

Above and opposite:
Various 1960s
Volkswagen ads.

Last one to conk out is a Volkswagen.

Whenever there's a bad rainstorm, we get some priceless publicity.

The newspapers often show a Volkswagen sloshing ahead in water up to its hubcaps while almost everyone else is waiting for the sun to come out.

We even have pictures of floating VWs. (We won't print them, though. Someone just might try to save a bridge toll and ferry his VW across a river. We don't recommend it.)

We do build the VW's bottom more like a boat than a car. But for a different reason.

We enclose the underside and seal it with rubber to protect all the working parts. Nothing is left exposed.

Every part of the Volkswagen from the bottom up is put together so well that the finished car is practically air-tight. (It should be. We've been improving and refining the same basic model for 15 years.)

If your Volkswagen ever does conk out in a flood, you can be sure of one thing.

You're in mighty deep water.

Repair 'em? I've got enough parts to build 'em!

There are 5,038 parts in a Volkswagen sedan and Dale Tuttle has all of them in stock or on tap. (So does every other authorized Volkswagen dealer.)

You don't wait to get a Volkswagen serviced. Mr. Tuttle repairs even vintage VWs with equal facility; their heart and face have remained the same.

Volkswagens parts are inexpensive. A new front fender is $21.75.* A cylinder head is only $19.95.*

Volkswagen service is fast (an engine can be removed and replaced in 90 minutes.)

If you lived in Bangalore, India, and ordered a Volkswagen we wouldn't deliver it. No VW service nearby.

VW spare parts are taken from regular production; identical with those in the car itself, and so just as good.

The intriguing thing is, they are seldom needed.

waste your money by buying the latest model every year just because the tail fins had been restyled. The Bug and the Bus would always look the same. There would be technical improvements, but they would be hidden. Americans, especially the younger ones, got it, and they started buying.

VW's ads encouraged America to question the endless promotion of keeping up with the neighbours. In fact, VW helped introduce America to an alternative way of thinking and living, which today we call the counter-culture.

26

WANTING THEM FOR EVER

Our VW occasionally stops working. And that's a surprise, because we love it so dearly, we sometimes take it too much for granted.

On a German autobahn near Brandenburg, a TDI Multivan has been playing up. Having a hi-viz jacket and warning triangle aboard is obligatory in many countries.

In the Moab Desert, Utah, a breakdown truck gives a tow while looking more decrepit than the hippy wagon it is there to rescue.

Near Tilos, Greece, someone's Beetle cabriolet has been obliged to wait far too long for roadside assistance.

All these VWs must be rescued, of course, including the cute one in Greece, condemned to advertise holiday apartments.

Opposite, above: A Beetle with greenery in Greece. Opposite, below: A rescue in Utah. Above: A rare breakdown in Germany.

27

RECYCLED VW

We lived just a field away from a car breaker's yard when I was a kid. My mate Maurice Walmsley lived in a house at the front of the yard because his dad owned the cars at the back. Oh, the joy of sitting in the driving seat of a long-deceased Jag with grass growing through the floor.

Here in New South Wales, Australia, is a Beetle graveyard. Long since stripped for spares, just the bodies remain. That was recycling then.

Today's deceased cars go to the crusher to emerge as blocks of metal, awaiting melt-down. The strange thing is, there is nothing actually wrong mechanically with many of them. Modern engines are built to such exact tolerances that they go on and on, and bodies do not rust, thanks to galvanising and hot-dipping. They are simply here because crucial electronic parts have failed and are uneconomic to replace.

But even this will become a thing of the past. VW designs with recycling in mind, so their cars' constituent parts will go their separate ways when the time comes.

Walmsley's crackers-up yard, as my mother called it, disappeared long ago. If it was there today it would be a Sustainable Auto-Recycling Centre. And that means nowhere for a kid obsessed with cars to dream.

28

RESTORED OR CONSERVED VW?

We owners demonstrate love for our pride and joy through restoring our classic VW to its youth. We say we chose this car because it is a model we always admired, or wanted when we were young, or actually owned or our dad owned. Maybe all of these.

But any psychologist will tell you why we really restore. As we cannot remove half a century of wear and tear from ourselves, we do so on our Beetle or camper van. Those years just melt away when we climb into that driving seat.

It's odd restoring an old car to new, or to what is called in the trade *concours condition*. We don't do that to ancient buildings, where the name of the game is conservation. Yet in recent times, things have been changing in the classic car world. A so-called *barn find*, code for a ratty wreck, can now be worth more with less intervention.

My own view is that the patina of age adds character (as of course it has with me – not). Restoration should therefore be directed to the mechanicals, so your classic VW can be driven safely. As for bodywork and interior, repair the bits that are unsafe, because you cannot have pieces of rusty metal hanging off, or seats that collapse.

Here are two examples of the different approaches. Unsurprisingly, the younger classic car owner tends towards conservation. It'll be interesting to know whether their views will change as they age themselves. I think perhaps not.

Opposite, above: A conserved VW Beetle.
Opposite, below: A restored VW Beetle.

29

THE DESIGNERS

We have seen that in 1925 a brilliant 18-year-old, Béla Barényi, was the first person, as far as we know, to come up with the design concept for what would become VW's first car.

Yet it was the Porsche design studio that finally put it into practice. This red 1936 prototype was designed by Erwin Komenda, a 'difficult' Austrian genius, who marched dangerously to his own tune. He dodged membership of the Nazi party, wouldn't address Hitler as 'Führer' or even give him the Nazi salute. After the war, Komenda was chief designer for Porsche, including the 911, a car he fell out with the Porsche family over, for they did not want it. Luckily for them, Erwin Komenda prevailed.

Other than Komenda, the person who had the greatest influence on the look of a VW must be Giorgetto Giugiaro, designer of the first Golf,

Above: VW Beetle prototype by Erwin Komenda. Opposite, left: Giorgetto Giugiaro with his first Golf in 1974. Opposite, right: Luigi Segre presenting the Karmann Ghia to Wilhelm Karmann's wife, 1955.

seen here in 1974 with his iconic creation. Yet neither man was the
product of the Bauhaus, that pre-war German school where form had to
follow function, meaning that science and art should be seen as one.

There have been many great designers employed at VW. Several
have studied automotive design at that child of the Bauhaus, London's
Royal College of Art. Which may explain the laid-back look of most VWs,
a look we love.

As for Luigi Segre's brilliant Karmann Ghia, that 'triumph of aesthetics
over common sense', there stands the exception that proves the rule.
Here on 14 July 1955, at the Kasino Hotel, Westphalia, Germany, is Frau
Wilhelm Karmann, wife of its German manufacturer, being shown the car
by Segre, owner of Carrozzeria Ghia.

'Bellissima,' he whispers. About the car?

30

HIPPY DIPPY VW

Where lies the spiritual home of the VW Camper Van, the Microbus, the Bus? It has to be California, specifically San Francisco. Here the 'turn on, tune in, drop out' movement started when Timothy Leary published his book with that title in 1966. The following year, 30,000 hippies gathered to see and hear the guru in Golden Gate Park, San Francisco at The Human Be-in. 'Abandon the established ways and stop conforming,' thundered Leary. Since then the VW Bus has retained its title as the undisputed hippy-dippy wheels of choice for all counter-culture, alternative types.

Here is one in Grant Avenue, China Town, San Francisco. Actually, it's a company bus owned by San Francisco Love Tours, which bills itself as 'The Original VW Hippie Tour'. So if you are a conventional type, this tour is for you.

In *Taking Woodstock,* a 2009 musical comedy about the 1969
Woodstock Festival, directed by Ang Lee, the actors Kelli Garner, Paul
Dano and Demetri Martin ham it up as hippies in the back of a VW.

What were these 1960s kids dropping out from? The Vietnam War,
for one. Or, just as important, the pristine, suffocatingly immaculate
lives of their post-war middle-class parents, anxiously competing in the
American Dream. An example has been recreated in this 1959 T1 Type 2
Westfalia Camper, a time when those hippy-dippies really were kids.

Actually, I'd rather like this Bus myself.

Above: A still from
Taking Woodstock
(Ang Lee), 2009.
Opposite: 1960s style
in a VW camper van.

1937–1939

1939–1945

1945–1948

1948–1960

1960–1967

1967–1978

31

THAT LOGO

No one knows for certain who first came up with the VW logo. It could have been Franz Reimspiess, the designer of the Beetle engine, or more likely Nikolai Borg, a graphic designer, or Martin Freyer, an artist. Here is how it has changed over the years.

VW logos over the years.

1978–1989

1989–1995

1995–2000

1999–2000

2000–2012

2012–2020

2019–Now

32

THE VW FAMILY

Do VW's designers ever feel constrained by the restrained, laid-back requirement of a VW? If so, they could go to work for another member of the VW family.

The 2020 blue Škoda Superb is a derivative of the VW Passat and is named after the pedigree Superb, built by the Czech company Škoda as a luxury automobile between 1934 and 1949. Škoda has a history far longer than VW. Dating back to 1859 as an armaments manufacturer, they started making cars in 1905. After the Second World War came the communist embrace of Czechoslovakia. Slowly the company's output became a standing joke:

What do you call a Škoda with a sunroof? Answer: A skip! (dumpster in US English).

The collapse of the Soviet empire allowed the company to be privatized in 1991 and Škoda became a full subsidiary of VW in 2000.

The red 2021 SEAT Ateca is a crossover SUV from the Golf SV and T-Roc stable. The Ateca is named after a Spanish village not far from SEAT's Barcelona headquarters. Actually it isn't produced in Spain at all, but in a Škoda factory in the Czech Republic. It shows how lines are deliberately blurred between family members and indeed countries when it comes to VW's worldwide production.

But if that's confusing, how about the Cupra brand, a subsidiary of a subsidiary – in this case SEAT? Here, in 2021, is a bluish Cupra UrbanRebel. The VW Group's designers must have loved having a go with this concept car.

Opposite, above: The 2020 Škoda Superb. Opposite, left: The Seat Ateca, 2020. Opposite, right: The Cupra UrbanRebel, 2021.

Above: The Bentley
Continental, 2021.
Left: The Lamborghini
Aventador, 2017.
Opposite, left: The
Bugatti Veyron.
Opposite, right: The
Bugatti Chiron at the
Goodwood Festival of
Speed, UK.

Then we move to Lamborghini. In 2017, this Aventador ignored the red traffic cone and pulled up for some traditional pie and mash in London's Camden Town. Cool place. Cool car. While in London, but now at the posh end, where better to park your Bentley Continental in 2021 than right outside your classic Knightsbridge townhouse? Dream on.

Let's go insane. Take this silver-plated Bugatti Veyron in the VW Autostadt Museum, Wolfsburg. Bling or what? It would do 254mph (400 km/h). But that's nothing. Here is VW's Bugatti Chiron. It can pull over 300mph (480 km/h). The question is, do these family members celebrate the real spirit of VW? I'm not too sure, even though many have interchangeable parts with VW itself.

So what is the real spirit of VW? Practicality? Lack of unnecessary decoration? Reliability? Unassuming appearance? Does what it says on the can? Drive forward, Porsche, such as the Taycan electric in 2023. This is the true child of the original Beetle, both born in the Porsche studio, one before the war, one after. What did Enzo Ferrari say of the Porsche? 'It's not a sports car. It's a projectile.'

33

THE FRONT END

What is characteristic about the front end of VWs? Not much, you may say.

Correct! A VW never makes a strong visual statement with its radiator grille. Of course, the original VWs – Beetles, Type 2 Microbuses, Karmann Ghias, didn't have a radiator.

This yellow 1974 Beetle is one of the last of the breed. What distinguishes this car is its unmistakable shape.

Fast-forward nearly half a century to this white ID.3. Looks familiar? Clean lines up front, but this time a big VW badge to distinguish it from every other look-alike make.

Opposite: The VW Beetle, 1974. Above: The VW ID.3, 2019.

34

THE LAID-BACK SIDE

In 1965 Donovan sang, 'Yellow is the colour of my true love's hair, In the morning when we rise ... That's the time I love the best.' I always think of his track 'Colours' whenever I see a yellow Type 2 VW Bus, such as this one in California, complete with appropriate props. Unlike other cars, the side view of most VWs celebrates a complete lack of styled aggression. It signals the simple life – no fuss, no show, no rush, just get where you're headed and enjoy.

That's also the message in this ID. Buzz, with its nostalgia-modern look, creating a distant echo of the Type 2. Here at an exhibition launch, it stands with a large photo behind of those wide-open spaces it's going to get away to. With all those charging points. Not that we care, because VW types are laid-back. So now Donovan's 'Mellow Yellow' is springing to mind.

Above: A Type 2 Bus.
Opposite: The ID. Buzz.

Above: The VW XL1.
Opposite: The ID.3.

35

THE REAR END

Here is the rear end of an ID.3 complete with a Norwegian licence plate. Norway was prudent enough to invest its North Sea energy, unlike the UK, which spent it, and Norway also now leads the UK by a long shot when it comes to installing a network of charging points – even into the Arctic. That is impressive.

As is this rear end. The profile of the licence-plate recess is reflected exactly in the rear-door opening. Few car designers do this top to bottom at the front and the rear – typically VW-esque, which means understated.

Not the VW XL1. Back in 2013, the fuel consumption on this hybrid 800cc two-cylinder turbo-diesel/electric was 300 miles (480km) per gallon. Only 250 were built, but only 200 people went out and bought one. It could have been the XL1's ticket price of £98,000 (over $110,000). Or was it also because, even if they could afford it, did VW types really want to drive around in a car with a rear end like this?

36

UP ABOVE

Cars aren't designed to be seen from up above. When do you ever study yours from such a vantage point, other than sticking your head out of a window to see if you are about to get a parking ticket below?

Luckily there is no warden in sight, so now you can notice how your car's front end has shrunk. The windshield seems to be hogging the space just where you thought the engine should be.

Why has this happened? It's nothing to do with fashion but everything to do with collision safety requirements and wind-tunnel testing. Safety and economy are the leading car designer concerns nowadays.

Yet a car's underpinnings are certainly a lot more complicated than in the past. Especially an electric one. Here is an ID.3, before it gets dressed.

Opposite, above and below: A VW ID.3.

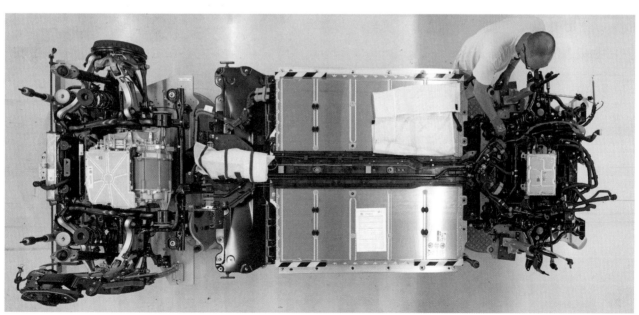

37

THE COCKPIT

Any VW looks purposeful inside. From the Beetle to the Golf to the ID range, you feel, when you are driving a VW, that you are sitting in a well-designed machine that is designed to get you where you want to go efficiently and without fuss or frills.

At night, a low glow from the instrument panel, as seen in this 2011 Golf GTI heading for Munich.

And straightforward buttons as seen in this 2020 Golf GTI. START ENGINE STOP. No bullshit. Just like VW owners.

Opposite: A Volkswagen
dashboard at night.
Above: Start button,
2020 VW Golf GTI.

38

CABRIO ZEITGEIST

From the very beginning there was a cabriolet VW. Think of that launch back in 1938. Actually, Hitler was presented with the very first, not that the Nazi faithful saw him using it in parades. He preferred a Grosser Mercedes.

After the war, the cabrio was reintroduced by VW, most being designed and built by the celebrated coachbuilder Karmann. That went on until 1979, making these cars the last Beetles to be built in Europe. Karmann also made the cabriolet version of the Karmann Ghia.

There were other Beetle cabrios, such as the one designed by coachbuilders Hebmüller, seen here in this 1949 version. These are pretty rare nowadays. Like the Karmann, you can see they are Beetle-derived.

Opposite: Cabriolet
VW Beetle. Above:
Hebmüller Beetle
cabriolets from 1949.

Above: The 1956
Rometsch Beeskow
cabriolet. Right: The
1953 Dannenhauer
cabriolet.

Not so with the even rarer Dannenhauer & Stauss and Rometsch interpretations. Unless you are a learned Beetle nut, you would be forgiven for thinking the Dannenhauer is an early Porsche. Here is a 1953 Dannenhauer and a 1956 Rometsch Beeskow.

VW has never recaptured the zeitgeist of their old cabrios. This 1990s Golf is a great car to drive, except does it have the elegant, understated finesse of a cool cabriolet? Then there was the Eos. No comment. And now we have the T-Roc SUV cabrio. Great to drive, but certainly no ballerina of a car.

Other marques have delivered the cool, timeless cabrio thing. Think BMW with their understated 3 Series, Mercedes with their legendary W124 and Saab with their sexy 900. Come to think of it, VW own Audi and Audi cabrios haven't all been bad-looking – some have been really cool.

So why aren't there VW versions? Working with a great coachbuilder, they need to get that VW Zeitgeist back. In fact, there's a name for a new VW cabriolet.

39

THE WHEELS

All VW wheels have a lot in common. Since the war, and probably more than any other marque, they have nearly always had a VW logo proudly on the hub. So here is a collection.

At the 2009 Gardening Scotland festival, in Ingliston, Edinburgh, a Beetle entry called 'Perennial Petal Power'. That's 'petal', not 'petrol'. It was made by students of Oatridge College, West Lothian, in aid of a retired gardeners' charity, for which its designers, Ann Burn and John Smith, won a Gold Medal.

And then, a simple cream 1955 Beetle at an Oxfordshire VW show in 2017. Very understated, but says it all.

In St Petersburg, Russia, in 2019, a Multivan California Ocean Bulli, or T6 to you and me. I like the reflection. Is that the Neva River in the distance?

In 2017, a Golf with wheels proudly announcing this GTI's performance capability, even when standing still.

Last but not least, a polished metal VW logo to which the eye is drawn, thanks to the design of the wheel. The best of this lot?

40

FASTER THAN YOU THINK

VW built its reputation on build quality and reliability although, as we've said, you could drive your KDF Wagen all day at a staggering *Mein Gott!* of 62mph (100 km/h). No comparable mass-manufactured car could do that in 1938 or even in 1968, when a Type 3 could slog on at 85mph (135 km/h) all day.

Yet it wasn't until the GTI came along that VW really got into cracking performance to add to its legendary dependability. That meant not just their old flag-waver of 'top speed = cruising speed', but acceleration, road-holding, braking and, dare I say, fun. The GTI not only broke new ground for VW but also gave the company a new image. They would exploit that with spin-off performance cars such as the Corrado VR6 Storm, and between 1988 and 1993 would fit their boy-racer G40 and G60 supercharged engines into certain of their hot hatches.

The VW Group has more to draw on than any other mass car manufacturer when it comes to performance. Think of their Audi, Bentley, Lambo and Bugatti brands. Behind all this lurks Porsche, VW's paterfamilias and guardian of the flame. Especially when it comes to performance. So it will be interesting to see what the future holds when it comes to sporty electrics.

The Golf R 333.

Normally VW, like other German manufacturers, have 155mph (250 km/h) limiters on their fastest cars. But with the limiter off you can reach 168mph (270 km/h) or maybe more in a Golf R 20 Years (shown on page 127), named to celebrate 20 years of the R models. The 20 Years has an EA888 turbocharged two-litre petrol engine and 328bhp, and is the last of VW's internal combustion engine high-performance cars.

Well, not quite. The new limited-edition Golf R 333 has even more bells and whistles. With the 333 you can have any colour provided it is Lime Yellow. Not that VW mellow yellow of yore. Inside you'll get Nappa leather sports seats and a Harmon Kardon top-of-the-range audio system, not forgetting a small numbered plaque to introduce the limited-edition tale to your envious passengers. Oh yes, and the 333 has a throaty Akrapovič exhaust system so they will know you are coming. The few being built were snapped up in eight minutes. Who said VW owners despise flash?

As for VW's go-faster future, it will be X-rated electric. So the sound of an Akrapovič exhaust system will be the final flourish. Just like the clatter of VW's air-cooled engines as they hammered in their millions down the world's autobahns, it will become a thing of the past. Oh well.

Opposite: The VW
Polo at the World Rally
Championship, Wales.
Below: *Irene-Ruby* out
and about with her
owners in the Welsh
countryside.

41

MALES IN WALES

A recent YouGov survey poll, held across Britain by carshop.co.uk, discovered that the average VW driver is aged 40 to 59, works in business, construction or finance, is a bit right of centre politically, likes high-end brands such as Marks & Spencer, Waitrose, Apple, British Airways (and, we assume, VW), is an efficient, hard-working chap and can also be a demanding perfectionist. He tends to be found in Wales.

This seems a little misleading and, in any case, possibly stereotypical. Here in Wales are VW Motorsport drivers Andreas Mikkelsen and Ola Fløene with their Polo R in the FIA World Rally Championship. Obviously these two are efficient, hard-working, demanding perfectionists, but even so, there must be lots of different males in Wales who aren't and who also favour VWs.

And another thing. VW and males do not always go together in Wales. Here is *Irene-Ruby*, a beautifully maintained 1971 camper van, which has brought much enjoyment to its owners, simply by pootling around Wales.

42

THE COLOUR

Why is it you don't see many VWs in bright colours nowadays? Not like this line of classic Beetles. Today everyone seems to choose dull colours like these Golf GTI guys in Switzerland, albeit with their lowered suspension and fancy wheels. Actually, you *can* get more pizazz in the look as well as the drive if that is what you want. But maybe you just have to go sober-sides when it comes to colour. Do you really want to be conspicuous when you are out there hot-hatching?

Above: Monochrome Golfs in Switzerland, 2018.
Opposite: A row of brighter Beetles.

43

THE ENGINES

VW has a proud history of engines dating back to that pre-war air-cooled model, designed by Franz Reimspiess of the Porsche studio. VW turned out these engines with, in VW-speak, 'progressive refinements', right into the early 21st century.

The first post-war cars had 1131cc engines giving 25bhp, but in 1953 the size was increased to 1192cc giving 30bhp. It was popularly called the 1200 engine and here is one. It was progressively refined into the 1300, 1500 and 1600 engines and those flat suitcase versions including 1700 and 1800s.

Today there are companies across the world making a good living building, reconditioning or enlarging these engines for enthusiasts, including VW car club members, dune buggy dudes and builders of eccentric flying machines. Most customers, however, are those you don't hear about very much, still using their air-cooled VW for work rather than fun, especially in Latin America.

Moving forward, here is a 2018 Golf GTI engine, polished and ready to go. Engines such as this are designed and built to such high tolerances that they are rarely the key unit failing first in an ageing car heading for the scrapyard. And neither is the rustproof body. That honour goes to the electronic bits.

So now to electric cars. Where is the engine? You tell me? The only engine we think about is the charging port, such as on this ID.7.

Which brings us back to the beginning – thanks to this ID Beetle.

Left, clockwise from top left: 1953 VW Beetle engine; Golf GTI engine, 2018; the charging port of an ID.7; a Beetle converted to electric.

44

SNOW VW

Driving up to a ski resort today, are you worried whether you will get there or not? Not really, because the roads are kept clear, and anyway, you are at the wheel of an SUV with all-wheel drive, or at least a front-wheel-drive car with the weight of the engine over your drive wheels.

Tackling snowy and icy roads wasn't that easy in the past. Which is why this 1960s black-and-white photo, with Grossglockner in the background, shows a car park almost full of VWs. And then there is a woman all ready to ski, with her white VW cabriolet in the Lechtal Alps in 1964. Ski gear looked like regular clothes in those days.

Volkswagens were excellent in snow and ice because they had their drive wheels under the engine, giving their cars grip. In some parts of the Alps, only a few marques of car, such as VW, Porsche and Saab, were allowed up in the winter. In America, the approach was different. Bags of sand or a tombstone in the trunk of your Oldsmobile could do the trick.

Above: VWs in an Austrian car park, 1960s. Opposite: Beetle with skis, 1964.

Wat voor wegen u ook neemt –

Hetzij een snelverkeersweg, hetzij een binnenweg, asfalt of kinderkopjes – zomer of winter, hitte of kou: deze wagen rijdt altijd en overal (als elke Volkswagen).
Dat heeft zijn oorzaak. Eén?
Dat heeft vele oorzaken!
Hij is luchtgekoeld (als elke Volkswagen). Hij heeft geen radiateur en geen koelwater nodig.
Geen antivries en geen garage. Realiseert u zich eens, wat dat betekent.

Zelfs wanneer u dagenlang met hem door de gloeiende Sahara rijdt – niets kan gaan koken. Want lucht kookt niet.
Of neem een tocht naar de ijzige Noordpool.
Niets kan kapotvriezen.
Omdat lucht niet bevriezen kan.
Of u nu de weg over de Grossglockner neemt of de steilste alpenpas berijdt, u behoeft onderweg nooit te stoppen om de motor te laten afkoelen. (Misschien alleen, omdat iemand om die reden juist moest stoppen).

zelfs met ijs of sneeuw

De Volkswagen-bus heeft de stuur- en veereigenschappen van een VW-personenwagen.
Onafhankelijke wielophanging en onafhankelijke vering met torsiestaven.
Verder dubbelwerkende telescoopschokbrekers en een grote bandenmaat.
Resultaat:
aangenaam rijden, een voortreffelijke wegligging.
Een VW-bus vertoont geen neigingen tot deinen of zweven.

De lichte besturing is van een hydraulische stuurdemper voorzien. Resultaat: oneffenheden in het wegdek worden niet op het stuur overgebracht, voortdurende stuurcorrecties zijn overbodig.
U kunt aangenaam en onvermoeid rijden.
De krachtige remmen zijn ruim bemeten en reageren op de geringste pedaaldruk. Zo heeft u de wagen in elke situatie volkomen in de hand en kunt u op alle wegen goed rijden.
Ook als u het geen wegen meer kunt noemen . . .

This splendid 1960s ad of a Type 2 in the mountains shows it passing muster when the going gets slippery. Now the Type 2 is no longer just a delivery van, but a lifestyle accessory.

You could have tried combining skiing with driving if you had this VW snowmobile. Capable of 160mph (100 km/h), it was designed and built by Rolf Strasser back in 1970.

Today, you can learn from watching Volkswagen's Dealerteam BAUHAUS when it comes to sliding around in your own modern VW. Here is Sweden's Johan Kristoffersson and Norway's Stig Rune Skjæmoen in a Polo GTI RS doing their stuff at the World Rally Championship in Sweden in 2019.

Opposite: Snowy
Dutch VW advertising.
Right: Rolf Strasser's
VW snowmobile, 1970.
Below: Polo in the
snow at the World
Rally Championship,
Sweden, 2019.

45

THE LOVE BUG

By 1968, love was in the air in America, all thanks to the previous year's
Summer of Love. And because the VW Bug had a love-in image, which
was becoming mainstream, one day somebody in Hollywood thought,
'Why don't we make a movie about a VW Love Bug? Never mind about
love being in the air. We will have it actually flying through the air.'

At first, Hollywood lawyers thought they might get sued by VW for
copyright. They insisted that all VW signs be stripped off the Love Bug.
But then, a funny thing happened. VW sales in America happened to
be going through a downturn. So it was time for their Madison Avenue
guys to intervene.

In 1968, a 1963 Beetle called Herbie flew through the air in *The Love
Bug*; and in sequels and on screen and TV he carried on doing so until
2005's *Herbie: Fully Loaded*. Here he is doing his stuff in 1974's *Herbie
Rides Again*.

Today there are many Love Bug clubs for those wishing to relive
younger days. Which is something all we collectors of old cars are
doing, really.

46

RALLYING AND RACING VW

As we've seen, VW loved supporting rallying ahead of pure racing. They were not the only ones. BMW, for example, took a similar approach.

Why? I think it's simply because showroom punters of performance VWs can see more of a connection with a rally car than a racing car.

Except in 2015, suddenly VW pulled out of motorsport entirely, including the World Rally Championship they had won in 2013 and 2014, the Dakar Rally and even Le Mans. It was 'say sorry' time, thanks to their leading part in the emissions scandal. Having their cars burning the gas and the rubber was not a good look. But here is a Polo R flying over the famous Micky's Jump before all that, in Sardinia in 2013. Eat your heart out, Herbie.

A Polo R at the Rally
Italia Sardegna, 2013.

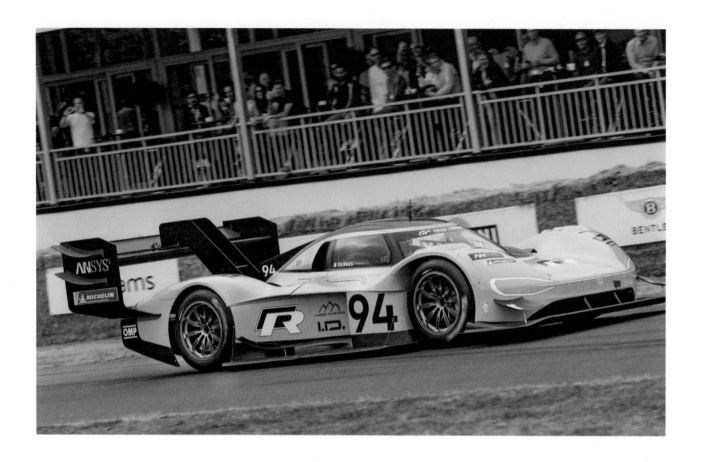

That's not to say that VW didn't back pure racing. This grey VW ID.R is being driven by Romain Dumas at the 2018 Goodwood Festival of Speed, while the blue ID.R was also at Goodwood the following year, also driven by Dumas but this time winning the Hill Climb.

Internationally, the ID.R is a Pikes Peak Hill Climb and Nürburgring record holder, and yes, it is electric. Indeed, it was VW's first electric racing car designed for motorsport competitions. Yet VW has announced it will no longer enter its VW-badged cars for motorsports, although it will continue with its premium brands, such as Audi and Bentley.

Above and opposite: ID.R electric racers at the Goodwood Festival of Speed, UK, in 2018 and 2019.

MEB 纯电动模块化平台

47

VW IN CHINA

VW entered China in 1978 with the Santana (Passat). Apart from being the first, VW is now the largest and most successful foreign car maker in the country. Today, China is VW Group's most profitable market, accounting for over 50 per cent of its global sales.

VW's main joint ventures are with SAIC (Shanghai Automotive Industry Corporation), where VW's holding is 40 per cent of the stock, and FAW (First Automobile Works), where its holding is 30 per cent.

Here in Chengdu in 2014, together with assorted Chinese and German officials, is Chancellor Angela Merkel. She is conversing with Xu Jianyi, president of FAW, about how the FAW production processes work.

In Anting, Shanghai, the SAIC joint venture dates back to 1984. The Shanghai plant is now concentrating on the production of electric VWs. On arrival, the visitor is greeted with the sculpture-like underpinnings of an electric vehicle mounted on a plinth. MEB stands for Modularer E-Antriebs-Baukasten or Modular Electric Drive Matrix. VW shares modular electronics across all its vehicles built here.

Opposite, above: Chancellor Angela Merkel at the First Automotive Works, Chengdu, China, 2014.
Opposite, below: Electric vehicle chassis on display at the Shanghai VW plant.

Right: The Wolfsburg
coat of arms, pictured
on a VW Beetle.
Opposite: The looming
VW chimneys of
Wolfsburg.

48

HQ VW

The German town of Wolfsburg is a pleasant place to live and raise a family. It is a pity they have built that huge factory next to it, with its four power-station chimneys looming over the residents.

That Wolfsburg is a pleasant place may well be true, but the rest isn't. The factory gave rise to the town, founded on 1 July 1938 as Stadt des KdF-Wagens bei Fallersleben or 'Town for the Strength Through Joy Car at Fallersleben'. At war's end, there were up to 15,000 enslaved labourers working in the factory.

In 1945, Major Ivan Hirst of the British Army took over both factory and town, now renamed Wolfsburg after the nearby Schloss Wolfsburg. Hirst changed the factory's name to Volkswagen, adopting the aristocratic coat of arms of the Schloss as an emblem for the VW Beetle.

Left: The vast Wolfsburg factory. Above: The Volkswagen Arena, home of the VfL Wolfsburg football team.

The power station was built in 1938 as the energy supplier for the factory designed by Ferdinand Porsche for the specific production of the KDF Wagen. After the war, despite its sinister beginnings, this huge building represented the resurgence and success of West German industry.

The panorama of the main factory and world headquarters shows its hugeness, so it's not surprising to discover that VW Wolfsburg is not only the largest automobile factory in the world but also, quite possibly, the largest factory in the world.

Wolfsburg also boasts a top-tier football team, VfL Wolfsburg, whose home ground is the Volkswagen Arena.

49

AUTOSTADT WOLFSBURG

Anyone entering Autostadt Wolfsburg, the Volkswagen Group's museum, will be struck by its sheer size and its sometimes whimsical nature, such as a robot carving out a model of a Golf.

It is a fascinating museum. Here you can take a walk through VW's history, view many other makes of car, connected or unconnected with VW, eat in one of the restaurants, watch a movie, take a boat trip on the Mittelland Canal, take a swim (if you are on the staff) and, at Christmas time, skate on the ice rink. Should you be collecting your new car, it will be delivered from a large glass silo tower.

Outside are cars displayed in large glass boxes, such as this 1951 VW Beetle. As we see, showing anything in a large glass box makes it an object of wonder, even a humble Beetle. If you'd like to see one displayed differently, there's an example on a plinth in the middle of the canal, which can be viewed more closely when you catch the boat trip.

Bringing the kids is fine. They won't get bored, especially in the electric dodgem Beetles, provided they've attended the safety briefing first. The photograph was taken in 2007, which means you are looking at some of VW's first all-electric cars.

For older kids – you and me – there are regular meetings in the Autostadtplatz for the world's VW car-club nuts, such as here in 2021. A great chance to see those Beetle rarities. How many can you identify?

Glass car silos in the Autostadt.

Opposite, above:
A Beetle on display at
the Autostadt.
Opposite, below:
Rare Beetles at an
enthusiasts' event.
Above: Dodgem
Beetles in the play area.
Right: A robot creating
a wooden model,
demonstrated at the
Autostadt.

50

I LOVE THESE CLASSICS

So, moment of truth. Which classic VWs would I keep in my garage, simply because I love them? It would have to be a 1970/71 Type 1 Beetle 1300 (which I have), a Type 2 Bay Window (which I prefer over the split screen – sorry!) and a 1978 Mk1 Golf GTI, displayed here in the Autostadt, Wolfsburg. And while I was at it, I'd throw in a family member – such as an early two-litre Porsche 911. Its designer, Ferdinand 'Butzi' Porsche (grandson of the founder), is looking on.

And if it was money no object, a limited-edition lithograph of *Lemon*, signed by Andy Warhol himself, to hang in my garage. Fully insured, of course.

Now, real world. Where did I put down those keyless keys to my ID.3?

Opposite, above:
Andy Warhol's *Lemon*
lithograph. Above: The
Porsche 911 2.0 Coupé,
1964. Right: 1978 Mk1
Golf GTI.

ABOUT THE AUTHOR

Vaughan Grylls is an artist and writer. He lives in London and East Kent and has been a VW enthusiast ever since he bought a 1956 Beetle in 1966. He has since owned more VWs than any other make of car.

ACKNOWLEDGEMENTS

This book would not have been possible without Rod Sleigh, Honorary President of the Historic Volkswagen Club, UK, for his valuable comments and advice on the technical aspects and history of VW, Magda Simoes-Brown at Batsford Books for sourcing many of the images, and Ferdy Carabott for resuscitating some ancient yet key ones. Last but not least, huge thanks to my editor Nicola Newman for keeping this book on the road.

INDEX

First published in the
United Kingdom
in 2024 by
Batsford
43 Great Ormond Street
London
WC1N 3HZ

An imprint of B. T. Batsford Holdings
Limited

ISBN 978 1 84994 875 3

A CIP catalogue record for this book
is available from the British Library.

10 9 8 7 6 5 4 3 2 1

Reproduction by Rival Colour Ltd, UK
Printed and bound by Toppan
Leefung Printing International, China

This book can be ordered direct
from the publisher at
www.batsfordbooks.com, or try your
local bookshop

PICTURE CREDITS

2, 92 Rosalind Simon/Alamy; 6–7 Lebrecht Music and Arts/Alamy; 8, 50 top Sue Thatcher/Alamy; 11, 24 bottom, 26 left and right, 44, 52 top, 52–53, 55, 58, 70, 76–77, 84–85, 117 top and bottom, 134–135 top and bottom, 146 top, 154 bottom dpa picture alliance/Alamy; 12, 23, 33, 66 top, 81, 86, 120, 136, 137 INTERFOTO/Alamy; 14 right UtCon Collection/Alamy; 16, 16–17, 20, 21 Shawshots/Alamy; 18–19, 150–151 Süddeutsche Zeitung Photo/Alamy; 22 Jeffrey Isaac Greenberg 8+/Alamy; 24 top, 110 Magic Car Pics; 27 Abaca Press/Alamy; 28, 112 John D. Ivanko/Alamy; 31 top Chas/Alamy; 31 bottom Kim Petersen/Alamy; 34 top, 38–39, 41 top and bottom, 48–49, 62, 123 left Phil Talbot/Alamy; 34 middle EnVogue_Photo/Alamy; 34 bottom Helissa Gründemann/Alamy; 36 Automotivia/Alamy; 40 imageBROKER.com GmbH & Co. KG/Alamy; 42, 124 bottom right, 132 Dmitrii Guldin/Alamy; 43 Sjoerd van der Wal/Getty Images; 47 Gruppo Editoriale LiveMedia/Alamy; 50 bottom Jim West/Alamy; 54 culture-images GmbH/Alamy; 57 top Andrey Artykov/Alamy; 57 bottom, 68 top Matthew Richardson/Alamy; 59 top Trinity Mirror/Mirrorpix/Alamy; 59 middle left WENN Rights Ltd/Alamy; 59 middle right Eugen Wais/Alamy; 59 bottom The Picture Art Collection/Alamy; 60–61 Ken Hurst/Alamy; 63 Ray Evans/Alamy; 65 top Ognyan Trifonov/Alamy; 65 bottom Malcolm Haines/Alamy; 66–67 Dipper Historic/Alamy; 66 bottom Wolfgang Spitzbart/Alamy; 67 Stephan Krudewig/Alamy; 68 bottom left Mark Eveleigh/Alamy; 68–69 Stephen Young/Alamy; 69 Peter Banos/Alamy; 71, 146 bottom Mark Andrews/Alamy; 72 top Robert W/Alamy; 72 bottom Taina Sohlman/Alamy; 73, 96 bottom Zuma Press, Inc./Alamy; 74 Roger Cracknell 01/classic/Alamy; 74–75 eddie linssen/Alamy; 75 57veedubs/Alamy; 79 Blackball Media/Alamy; 80–81 Alex Segre/Alamy; 80 bottom,

83, 158 Vaughan Grylls; 88–89, 134 top left Heritage Image Partnership Ltd/Alamy; 92 bottom Frontline Photography/Alamy; 93, 152, 155 bottom Agencja Fotograficzna Caro/Alamy; 95 top Ashley Cooper/Alamy; 95 bottom Marcus Harrison – environment/Alamy; 96 top Bryn Lerwill/Alamy; 98 Joern Sackermann/Alamy; 100–101 Helen 123/Stockimo/Alamy; 102 Cinematic/Alamy; 103 Dmitry Orlov/Alamy; 107 top, 107 bottom left VDWI Automotive/Alamy; 107 bottom right Santi Rodriguez/Alamy; 108 top Bong!/Stockimo/Alamy; 108 bottom Goddard on the Go/Alamy; 109 left Herb Bendicks/Alamy; 109 right UK Sports Pics Ltd/Alamy; 111 Svetla Momchilova/Alamy; 113 Vehicles/Alamy; 114 P Cox/Alamy; 115 Sergio Azenha/Alamy; 118–119 Peter Brierley/Alamy; 123 right Grzegorz Czapski/Alamy; 124 top left floralpik/Alamy; 124 top right Tim Gainey/Alamy; 124 middle right Clynt Garnham/Stockimo/Alamy; 124 bottom left CHROMORANGE/Karlheinz Pawlik/Alamy; 130 top PA Images/Alamy; 130–131 keith morris/Alamy; 133 Frank Heinz/Alamy; 134 bottom left Itsanan Sampuntarat/Alamy; 139 top Keystone Press/Alamy; 139 bottom TT News Agency/Alamy; 140 top Everett Collection Inc/Alamy; 140 bottom Mim Friday/Alamy; 142–143 Action Plus Sports Images/Alamy; 144, 145 pbpgalleries/Alamy; 149, 151 Ilari Näckel/Alamy; 154 top Ian Masterton/Alamy; 155 top Mark Daffey/Alamy; 156 © 2023 The Andy Warhol Foundation for the Visual Arts, Inc. / Licensed by DACS, London; 157 top Goddard Archive Portraits/Alamy; 157 bottom Aliakseu Matsiushkou/Alamy. All reasonable efforts have been taken to ensure that the reproduction of the content in this book is done with the full consent of the copyright owners. If you are aware of unintentional omissions, please contact the company directly so that any necessary corrections may be made for future editions.